GW01311370

Part of the Simple guide series

Some images credited: freepik

Written by Daniel Turner & Valerie M. Howell

Illustrator:
Daniel Turner & Victoria Volodina

This title is in United States English.

SIMPLE HISTORY

A SIMPLE GUIDE TO

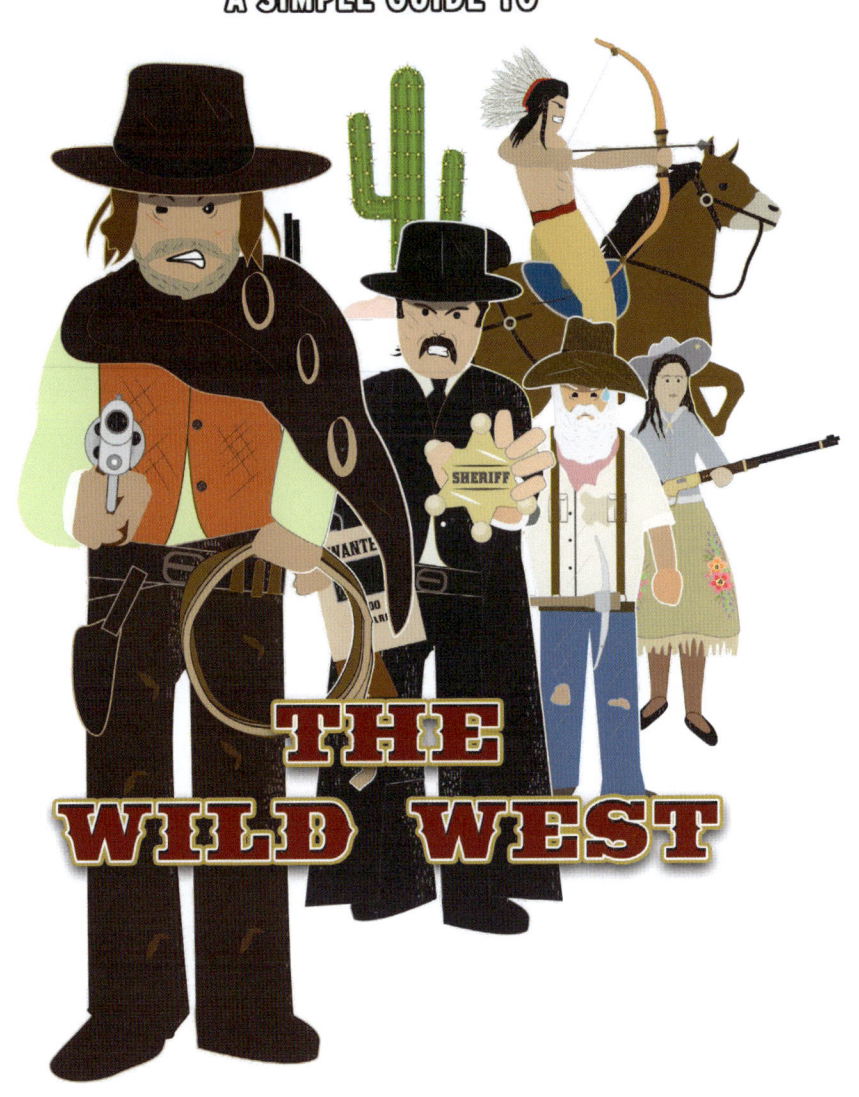

THE WILD WEST

Written by Daniel Turner & Valerie M. Howell
Illustrated by Daniel Turner

CONTENTS

INTRODUCTION

In the western part of the United States was a place known as the Wild West. In the desert and red rock valleys, cowboys, gunslingers, lawmen, gold miners and Native Americans were a part of the world that existed a long time ago. It was an exciting time that began with exploration of Lewis and Clark and ended with Wild West towns and cowboy shows. Along the way, a railroad connected the Pacific to the Atlantic, pioneers went west, towns were built and legends were made.

THE FRONTIER IS OPEN!

LOUISIANA PURCHASE

1803

The history of the American west began in 1803 when President Thomas Jefferson purchased the territory west of the Mississippi from France for $15 million. This is known as the Louisiana Purchase. This purchase doubled the size of the new nation known as the United States. In 1805, he sent two explorers, Lewis and Clark to explore the west. With the help of their guide Sacagawea, the expedition reached the Pacific Ocean.

The frontier was now open. The first Americans who went west were trappers and hunters. These men traveled westward and made their living trapping beavers and hunting game. They made friends with many Native American tribes. They explored many areas in the Rocky Mountains that had never been seen by Europeans before. They lived very simple lives in cabins and often had to depend upon themselves for survival. They were known as mountain men and some of their adventures became legend.

THE GOVERNMENT FORCES THE CHEROKEE TO MOVE WEST

1838

With so many millions of acres available in the west, the American Congress decided to pass the Indian Removal Act in 1830. This act put into law the removal of the all Native Americans from the United States to the West. In 1838, the entire Cherokee nation was forced from their lands in the southeast. They had no say and were not able to fight back. Men, women, children, old and sick were forced to walk over a thousand miles to the Oklahoma territory. Many died along the way. This was known as the Trail of Tears.

MANIFEST DESTINY

WEST ⟵

After the American Revolution, there began a movement westward. As the new nation of the United States grew from the original 13 states, a belief that it was the destiny of this new nation to grow its borders all the way to the Pacific Ocean grew and gained followers. By 1840, this belief became known as Manifest Destiny and shaped the west for decades to come. The United States Government encouraged farmers and ranchers to go west and settle the new land.

THE MEXICAN-AMERICAN WAR

1846 - 1848

As Americans moved west, there was growing tension in Texas. Texas was then part of Mexico and the Mexican government. Settlers who moved into the area called for Texas to become independent of Mexico. In 1836, Mexican troops attacked a mission known as the Alamo. There were many settlers in the Alamo who supported the fight for Texas' independence. It was a massacre with only two settlers surviving. Many settlers in Texas kept fighting with a rallying call of "Remember the Alamo". In 1846 Mexico and the United States fought a war over Texas. The United States won in 1848. For $15 million, the United States purchased the territory that spread from Texas to California from Mexico.

DAVY CROCKETT

David Crockett was born in 1786 in North Carolina which is now known as Tennessee. He was a politician and noted frontiersman. He opposed the Indian Removal Act. After losing his seat in Congress in 1835, he left for Texas. He took part in the Texas Revolution, where settlers opposed the Mexicans and fought for independence. He died at the Battle of Alamo in 1836.

THE OREGON TRAIL 1846

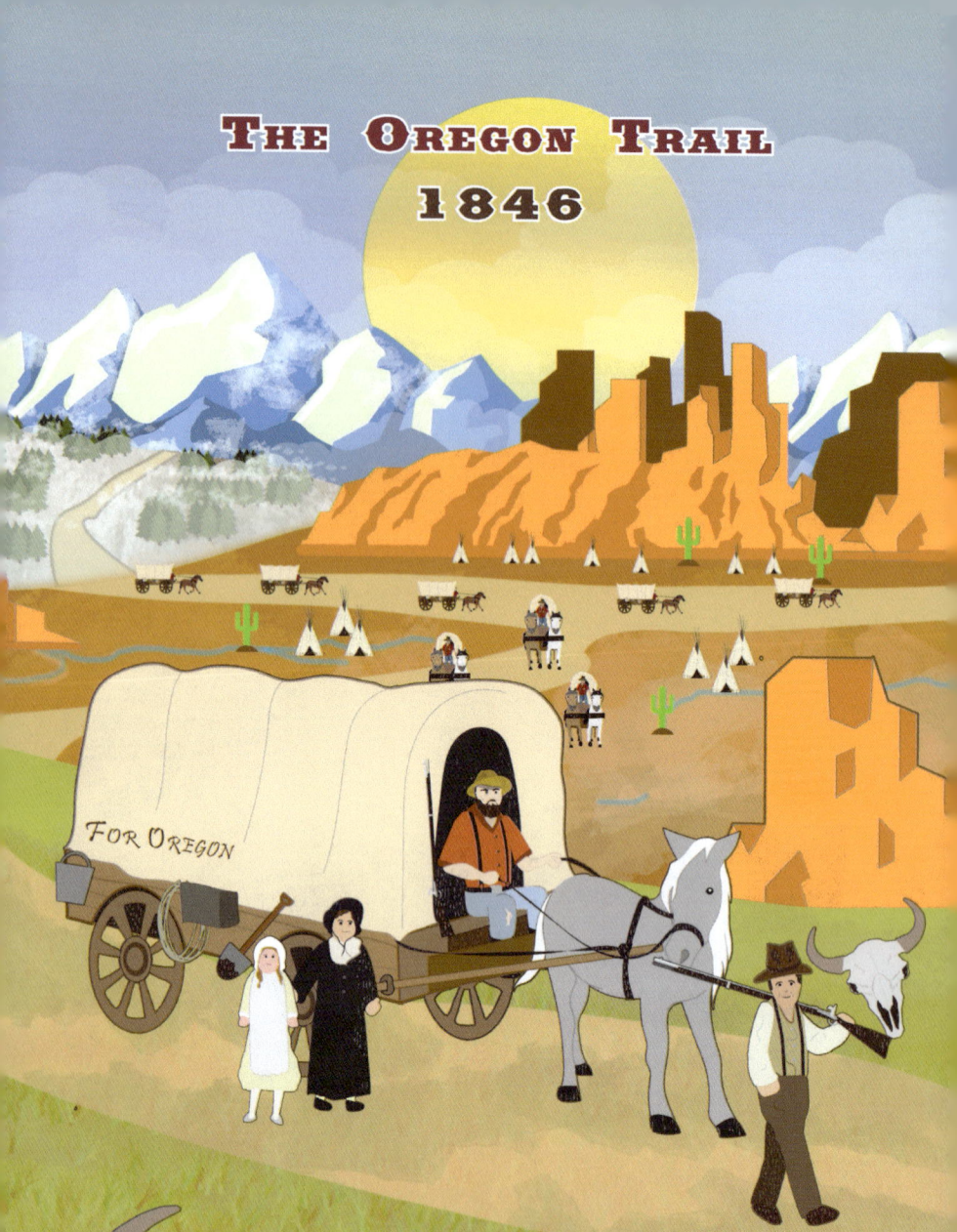

FOR OREGON

 1846 was a busy year. England gives the Oregon territory to the United States in the Oregon Treaty. Settlers start arriving in covered wagons over the Rockies and along the Oregon Trail. Brigham Young, the leader of the Mormon church leads 5000 followers to Utah with the hopes of establishing a community free of religious persecution. Thousands of settlers make the trip west.

THE GOLD RUSH BEGINS!
1849

In California, gold was discovered in 1848 and the country is soon consumed by gold fever as the gold rush begins. Thousands of men made their way through dangerous country or sailed around South America to come to California hoping to strike it rich.

Most of these new arrivals came during the year 1849, and they are known as the "forty-niners". The gold miners often lived in mining camps in terrible conditions.

THE SILVER BOOMTOWNS 1850s

During the 1850s, vast quantities of silver were discovered in Nevada, which led to the rise of boomtowns. These towns would become famous for their place in the lore and legend of the Wild West. Virginia City, Carson City and Silver City all were built as a result of silver mining.

THE MAIL ARRIVES!
1860

As settlers, gold miners and pioneers began heading west and the mail soon followed. In 1860, the Pony Express delivered mail to settlements and small communities along its route. These brave men would ride through the harsh and unforgiving landscape for days to deliver mail. In 1861 the Pony Express was replaced by the telegraph. The telegraph was cheaper, safer and faster than traditional mail.

THE HOMESTEAD ACT

1862

In the first few decades of the 1800's, the west was a wild place full of millions of miles of open range, forests, mountains and deserts. Many tribes of Native Americans called this place their home. There were no roads or railroad. It was a country that was full of resources and the American government wanted to make sure that pioneers from the East could settle it and take those resources for their own. In 1862, the Homestead Act was passed, which offered free land out west to farmers. Thousands of families headed West in covered wagons and traveled in wagon trains to start a new life.

THE RAILROAD LINKS THE ATLANTIC TO THE PACIFIC 1869

With the help of the funds from the government, the railroad linking the East Coast with the West Coast was finally completed. In 1869 the Transcontinental Railroad was finished in a little town called Promontory, Utah. With the railroad complete, more people were able to travel out West.

THE WILD WEST

Many towns in the Wild West became known for violence and greed. Miners with gold and silver in their pockets would mingle with cowboys and gunslingers. Law was upheld by sheriffs and a few lawmen. Many citizens followed their own code of law. This code developed in the west and allowed for the settling of disputes without the benefit of the courts. Often these disputes were settled by pistols and violence according to the law of the west.

COWBOYS AND CATTLE RANCHERS

Many parts of the west were not suited for farming but were perfect for cattle ranches. Thousands of miles of open range were ideal grazing lands for herds of cattle. Ranchers often hired men to guard the cows from cattle rustlers, or cattle thieves. The cowboys also rode the range protecting the herds from predators and ensuring that the herds would make it to market. The cowboy with his horse, spurs, pistol and hat became an iconic part of the legends of the Wild West.

WESTWARD EXPANSION LEADS TO TROUBLE

After the railroad was compete, more and more people came to the west to make their fortunes. Towns sprang up and cattle ranchers and farmers claimed large amounts of acres. Many times, these new farms and cattle ranches came into direct conflict with the lands and rights of the Native Americans. The United States Government made many treaties with the Native Americans and broke them all. This led to trouble.

BATTLE OF LITTLE BIGHORN

JUNE 25, 1876 – JUNE 26, 1876

By the 1870's the United States was waging war against the Native Americans of the West. Native Americans were killed and massacred. The buffalo that they depended on for survival were slaughtered by the thousands by the United States Cavalry with their new invention, the Gatling gun.

CUSTER'S LAST STAND

After fighting in the Civil War, he was sent to the west to help crush Native American resistance. He died at Little Bighorn.

So many buffalo were killed that the species neared extinction. The Lakota, Cheyenne and Arapahoe tribes joined forces in revenge and met the U.S. Cavalry led by General Custer on the battlefield at Little Big Horn. The Native Americans led by Sitting Bull and Crazy Horse won the day.

BILLY THE KID

Born in 1859 as Henry McCarty, Billy the Kid was a gunslinger by trade. He is one of the most famous gunslingers of the Wild West. He is known to have killed eight men but may have killed more. He lived a short life and died at the age of 21. The cause of death was a gunshot wound.

GUNFIGHT AT THE OK CORRAL
1881

In 1881 the most famous gunfight in the history of the Wild West happened in the town of Tombstone in the Arizona Territory. What began as a feud between a group of cowboys and lawmen including Wyatt Earp, and his brothers, Virgil and Morgan and their friend Doc Holliday turned into a 30 second gunfight. The gun fight took place near the OK Corral and ended in the death of cowboys, Billy Clanton, Tom and Frank McLaury. The cowboys, Ike Clanton and Billy Claiborne escaped and vowed to seek revenge. Virgil and Morgan Earp and Doc Holiday were all wounded during the fight. This gunfight became legend after Wyatt Earp's biography was published in 1931.

THE END OF AN ERA

 In the decades following the Battle of Little Big Horn, many Native Americans were rounded up and forced onto reservations. Settlers and pioneers had become prosperous farmers and cattle ranchers. Mining towns had grown into small cities or had been abandoned when the silver and gold dried up. Courts and law had been established firmly in many places. The territories were becoming states. The famous lawmen and the gunslingers faded into American legend or became part of Wild West shows. It was the end of an era.

THE WILD WEST SHOW

After it became tamed and not so wild, American audiences were fascinated by the idea of the Wild West. Traveling shows, very much like circuses, became popular in the 1880s. For the cost of a ticket, you could watch a shootout between cowboys and Indians. You could see a stagecoach get robbed or even watch cowboys perform daring stunts on horseback.

1880s

There were famous people like Anne Oakley and Wild Bill Hickok demonstrating their skills with a gun. It was a thrilling and fun way to relive the excitement of the Wild West without having to risk your life.

ANNIE OAKLEY

Born Phoebe Ann Mosey in 1860, Annie Oakley began her career as a sharp shooter at the age of 15 by winning a shooting match against famous sharpshooter, Frank E Butler. She later married him and together they joined Buffalo Bill's Wild West show. Her career as a sharp shooter spanned decades. She died in 1926.

LIFE IN THE WILD WEST

HOW TO MAKE A LIVING IN THE WILD WEST

HOW TO BE A PIONEER

The time is the 1850's and you want to go west and strike it rich. First you will need to buy a wagon and some horses. Be sure your wagon is sturdy and can hold everything you will need for your new life. You will need to carry food, supplies, clothes, and any furniture or belongings that you will need when you get to the Oregon territory. There are few general stores where you are going so you will not be able to buy something if you didn't bring it with you. Be sure you bring enough food for you and your horses to last for the six month journey of 2,000 miles on the Oregon Trail. Don't forget to bring your pistol and rifle so you can protect yourself from robbers and hunt for food.

How to be a Cowboy

You have decided to become a cowboy. You are going to need a few things to live on the range. The most important purchase will be your horse. A good, dependable horse is essential for your new job. You will need a pistol and a rifle. These will come in handy for protecting the herds from rustlers, predators and sometimes for defending yourself. You will want to spend money on a good saddle as you are going to be sitting in it for hours each day. You will need a hat to keep the sun out of your eyes and your face from getting sun burned. You will also need boots, spurs, chaps, a bedroll and a lasso for rounding up cattle.

How to be a Gunslinger

You have chosen to be a gun for hire. You are known for your skills with a pistol and you don't mind breaking a few laws. Besides, you adhere to a different set of laws, the laws of the West. You have chosen a profession that is very dangerous and will most likely result in your early death by a bullet or at the end of the hangman's noose. To be a gunslinger, your most important purchase will be your gun, or even two. You will need to know how to use it and shoot it faster than anyone else. You probably will not need many other things aside from your clothes and maybe a horse as you will probably not live very long.

How to be a Sheriff

In the lawless world of the Wild West, lawmen like you were few. You represented all the laws of the United States and its territories. In many places, you were the only officer. It was your responsibility to keep the peace in boomtowns and settle disputes without bloodshed. You were often the only person capable of bringing a lawless criminal to justice or protecting the townsfolk from harm. You will need a good set of pistols and a long rifle. You will also need clothes, boots, spurs, a reliable horse, and a hat.

How to be a Gold Miner

It is the 1840's and you have just heard the news, that gold was discovered in California! You decide that you want to head out west and strike it rich. Since you live in a state along the Atlantic Ocean, you have a long journey ahead of you. You will want to book passage on a boat which will sail thousands of miles around South America and back up to California. If you don't like boats, you can walk. It's only 2,000 miles once you reach St. Louis. Once you get to California, you will a need a tent, a bed roll, a pan, and a pick axe.

How to be a Plains Indian

You were raised on the lands of the Great Plains. Your tribe has followed the great herds of Buffalo for generations. You are nomadic and you hunt the buffalo that gives you everything you need to survive. Its hide clothes you and protects you from the elements. Its meat feeds you and its stomach makes bags and pouches. The fat can be burned or used for grease. Your people have depended upon the buffalo for survival and now that is threatened. Settlers put fences across the grazing land of the buffalo and the United Stated Cavalry kills the herds to starve you. Your people are in trouble and you are no longer sure of your place in this world.

THE SALOON

The saloon was an important part of life in the Wild West. Cowboys, gunslingers, gamblers, miners, travelers, and townspeople would gather at the saloon to socialize, play a few hands of cards and to relax. Some saloons served food and offered live music. Early saloons were often tents set up in mining camps with later saloons being wooden structures decorated with green velvet card tables, long bars, mirrors and chandeliers. Saloons were popular from 1870-1890 with over 33,000 documented across the west.

OPEN

THE BARKEEPER

Sometimes he was the owner or he worked for the saloon owner. He served drinks to the patrons. The drinks he served were usually homemade and very strong. These drinks had names like Tarantula Juice, Taos Lightning, and Coffin Varnish.

THE GAMBLERS

Card games were very popular in the Wild West. These games were often played for money. Gamblers were professional card players who traveled from town to town making their living from winning at cards. Gamblers would often try to win money from the cowboys and miners who were gullible enough to play cards with them. Gamblers would often find themselves in disputes so they also had to be handy with a gun.

The Cowboy

After weeks on the range, cowboys would come to town with the cattle, which would be sold at market. These men would go to the local saloon to have a few drinks, play some cards and relax after weeks of hard work.

The Entertainer

Some saloons offered live music. Often the music was provided by a piano player who was a singer, a musician and often a comedian. Traveling troupes of actors and actresses would perform music, comedy, or small plays as they traveled from town to town.

The Gunslinger

Gunslingers were guns for hire and would meet employers at saloons to conduct business. They also would meet other gunslingers at these establishments to settle disputes as to who was better or faster. These disputes would often be settled by duels.

DUELING IN THE WILD WEST

In the Wild West, there was law but it was enforced by sheriffs, marshals, and judges who were often responsible for very large areas. Disputes such as gambling or fights among gunslingers were often settled in duels. Dueling was a very old practice that began with the knights of medieval times and survived into the old west. This practice was part of the code of law of the Wild West. It was often honor based and had strict rules. One of the most popular forms of dueling was the Quick Draw which depended entirely on how fast a pistol could be pulled from a holster, aimed and discharged. Dueling became such a popular way of settling disputes that some towns passed laws prohibiting the carrying of firearms in public.

THE END

The Wild West was a place that existed in the western half of the United States from 1805 to the 1880's. It included cowboys and gunslingers, Indians and Cavalry, gold miners and sheriffs. It was a time and place that will forever capture the imagination. You can still visit it in movies and books.

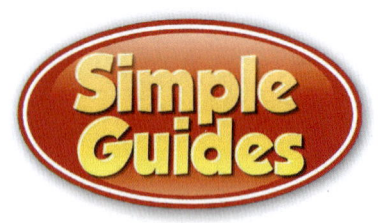

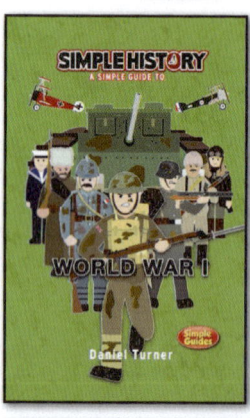

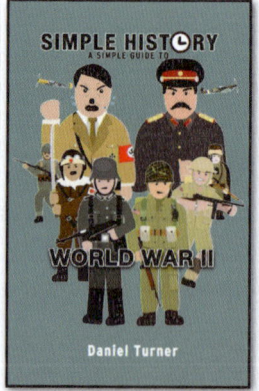

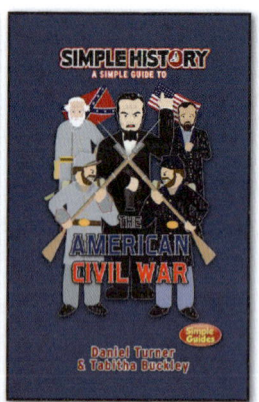

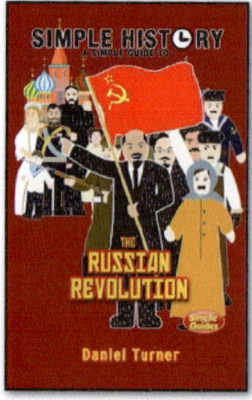

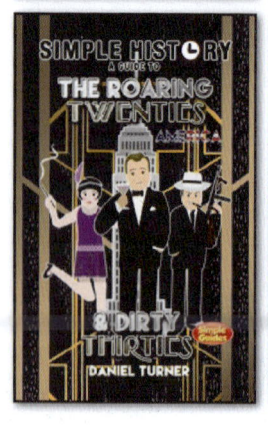

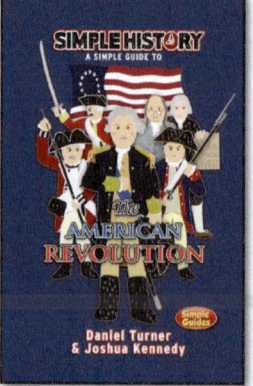

On tablet / phone   computer   print

In print, tablet and e-book formats

Sign up for the mailing list for Simple History news. Simply Scan the QR code to the left with your phone.

Visit the website and social media!

www.simplehistory.co.uk

Printed in Great Britain
by Amazon